hen

gallina

rooster

gallo

chick

pulcino

duckling

anatroccolo

turkey

tacchino

donkey

asino

swan

cigno

frog

rana

racoon

procione

bear

orso

squirrel

scoiattolo

fly

mosca

ladybug

coccinella

worm

verme

snail

lumaca

slug

lumacone

bee

ape

spider

ragno

beetle

scarabeo

dragonfly

libellula

lion

leone

zebra

zebra

giraffe

giraffa

rhinoceros

rinoceronte

snake

serpente

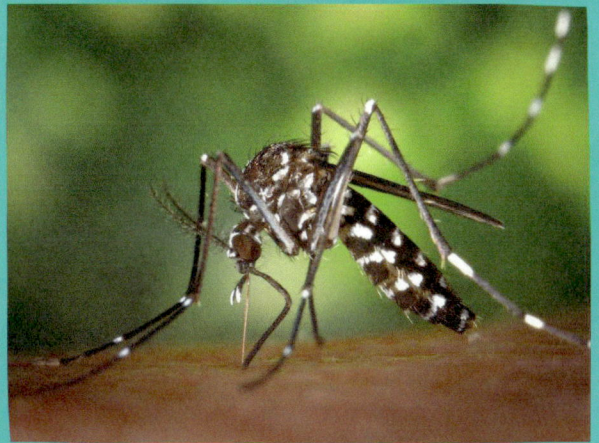

mosquito

zanzara

sea turtle

tartaruga marina

hippopotamus

ippopotamo

alligator

alligatore

crocodile

coccodrillo

shark

squalo

walrus

tricheco

penguin

pinguino

polar bear

orso polare

seal

foca

starfish

stella marina

jellyfish

medusa

seashells

conchiglie

feather

piuma

11

eleven

undici

12

twelve

dodici

13

thirteen

tredici

14

fourteen

quattordici

15

fifteen

quindici

16

sixteen

sedici

17

seventeen

diciassette

18

eighteen

diciotto

19

nineteen

diciannove

20

twenty

venti

heart

cuore

oval

ovale

arrow

freccia

crescent

mezzaluna

curve

curva

spiral

spirale

cross

croce

zigzag

zigzag

rainbow

arcobaleno

dark colors

colori scuri

light colors

colori chiari

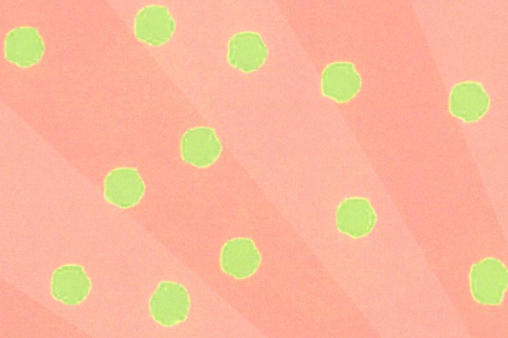 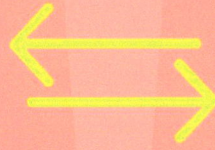 

dots

puntini

line

linea

short

basso

tall

alto

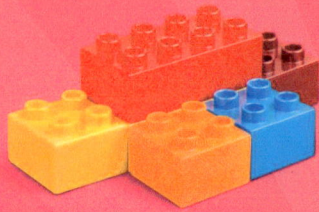  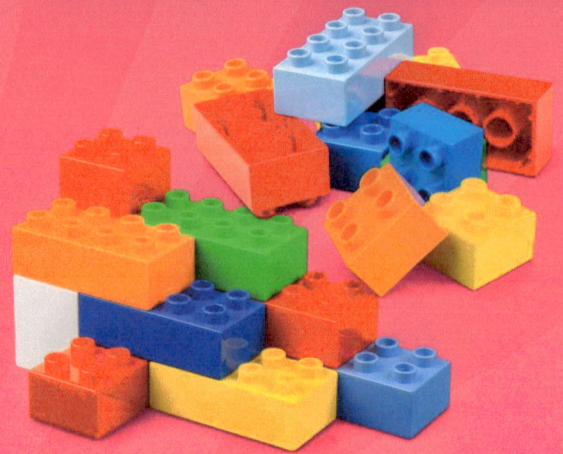

a little

poco

a lot

tanto

full

pieno

empty

vuoto

curly hair

capelli ricci

straight hair

capelli lisci

accept

accettare

refuse

rifiutare

identical

identico

different

diverso

dry

asciutto

wet

bagnato

toys

giocattoli

blocks

blocchi

ball

palla

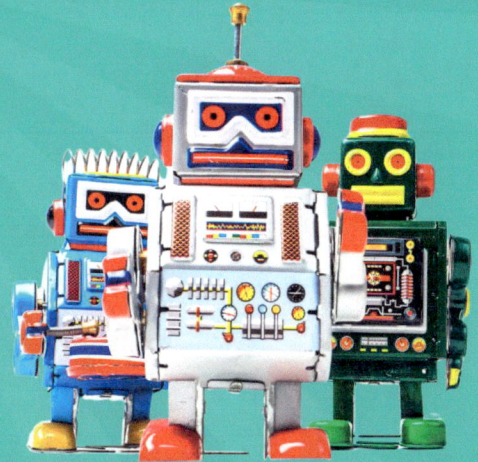

robots

robot

tongue

lingua

nose

naso

hair

capelli

moustache

baffi

fingers

dita

arm

braccio

knee

ginocchio

elbow

gomito

smile

sorridere

kiss

baciare

cry

piangere

pain

dolore

body

corpo

back

schiena

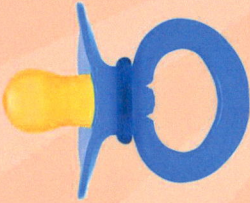

pacifier

ciuccio

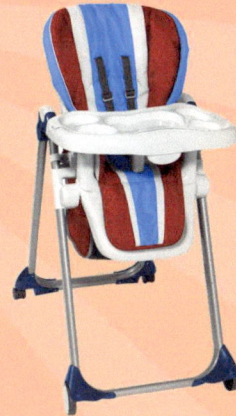

high chair

seggiolone

soap

sapone

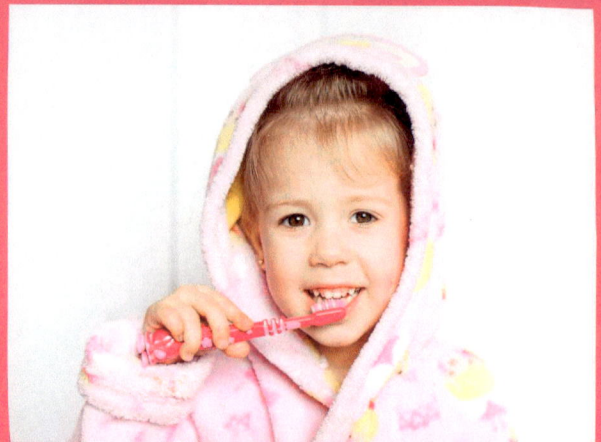

toothbrush

spazzolino

towel

asciugamano

potty

vasino

ring

anello

bracelet

bracciale

necklace

collana

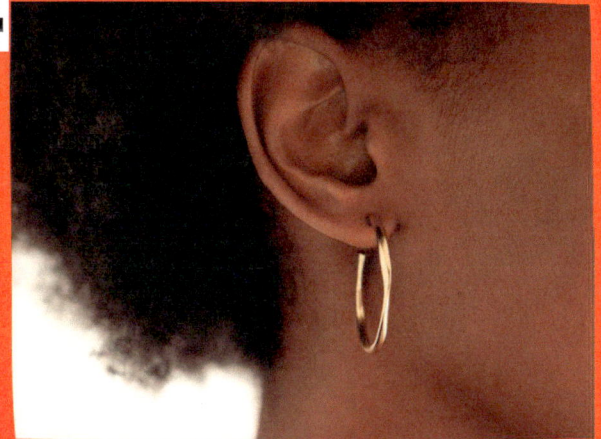

earring

orecchino

chocolate

cioccolato

popcorn

popcorn

jam

marmellata

toast

pane tostato

honey

miele

butter

burro

bread

pane

ice cream

gelato

semolina

semola

rice

riso

pasta

pasta

soup

minestra

milk

latte

water

acqua

juice

succo

kiwi

kiwi

raspberry

lampone

grapefruit

pompelmo

melon

melone

plum

prugna

apricot

albicocca

pomegranate

melograno

fig

fico

blueberry

mirtillo

cranberry

mirtillo rosso

persimmon

cachi

lychee

litchi

fruits

frutti

vegetables

verdure

avocado

avocado

green bean

fagiolino

broccoli

broccolo

eggplant

melanzana

peas

piselli

bell pepper

peperone

beet

barbabietola

lettuce

lattuga

endive

indivia

artichoke

carciofo

leek

porro

onion

cipolla

garlic

aglio

ginger

zenzero

walnuts

noci

almond

mandorla

pistachio

pistacchio

cashew

anacardo

Made in United States
Troutdale, OR
06/09/2024